COMMUNICATION AND CONFLICT MANAGEMENT:

A HANDBOOK FOR THE NEW DEPARTMENT CHAIR

—

By
J. Emmett Winn
Associate Provost and Professor
Auburn University

To order additional copies

Please call Academic Impressions' office at 720.488.6800 or visit www.academicimpressions.com/books

AUTHOR

J. EMMETT WINN
Associate Provost and Professor
Auburn University

As associate provost, Dr. Winn provides leadership on academic and administrative issues for Auburn's thirteen colleges and schools. In this capacity, Dr. Winn oversees processes related to faculty hiring, evaluating, and issues related to the promotion and tenure processes and post-tenure review. Dr. Winn works closely with the more than sixty department chairs, the university promotion and tenure committee, the university senate leadership, and all academic deans.

In addition to being Auburn University's associate provost, J. Emmett Winn is a professor in the Department of Communication and Journalism. Dr. Winn has served Auburn University for the past twenty years. Additionally, he is a longtime member of the AAUP and works with all campus constituents to ensure the institution's commitment to shared governance.

HIGHER ED IMPACT

Delivered free to your inbox, Higher Ed Impact provides you with a full tool kit to help you monitor and assess the trends and strategic challenges likely to have an impact on your institution's health and competitiveness.

DailyPulse

Scan current events, timely research, and notable practices at other institutions.

WeeklyScan

Review the week's most significant events and the most timely research in higher education, with key takeaways suggested by higher education's leading experts.

Diagnostic

Get an enterprise-wide and in-depth look at a current, strategic challenge; identify steps to take and critical questions to address.

Learn more or sign up to receive Higher Ed Impact at: www.academicimpressions.com/news-sign-up

Meeting the Challenge of
Program Prioritization

About Academic Impressions

We believe that higher education is the engine of the American dream.

To remain accessible and affordable, the higher-ed business model must be made more sustainable. We believe these changes are within the industry's control, and we believe we can help.

Each year we serve thousands of colleges and universities through professional development, research, and publications. AI is not a policy organization. We foster innovation and focus on what can be done today. We address, head-on, the unique and difficult challenges higher education faces.

OTHER BOOKS YOU MAY ENJOY

Evacuation Planning Procedures for Study Abroad Emergencies
www.academicimpressions.com/evacuation-planning-proce-
dures-study-abroad-emergencies

As study abroad programs grow in higher ed, so too does the need for
crisis planning. This guide will walk you through many scenarios and
how to resolve them, and will review:

- 5 critical steps to developing an effective evacuation plan

- Tools and checklists for on-site protocols in the event of a medical
  evacuation, a natural disaster, or political unrest

- How to ensure clear communication during the response and
  evacuation

- How to determine the appropriate response to the event

- What to expect regarding the costs of evacuation

- How to respond to media inquiries effectively

Fundraising for Deans: A Guide
https://www.academicimpressions.com/monograph/fundrais-
ing-deans-guide

Read this guide for an innovative primer on:

- How the dean can take a lead role in defining the case for support
  and identifying inspiring projects defined by specific objectives
  rather than by categories of need

- The respective roles and responsibilities of the dean, faculty, and the
  college development staff

- How deans can work most effectively with the president, the central
  advancement office, and their development officer

- The dean's specific role in donor stewardship, campaigns, volunteer
  management, and making the ask

Table of Contents

INTRODUCTION

Effective communication is more difficult than it sounds, yet essential to the department chair position—it will make or break a department chair. Surveys conducted by Robert E. Cipriano and Richard L. Riccardi over a period of seven years with more than five hundred responses from department chairs from across the United States show that the chairs themselves ranked communication as one of their top three essential skills (along with budget skills and the ability to effectively evaluate faculty).

The truth is that interacting with the broad group of faculty, staff, students, alumni, and others who make up academic departments, schools, and colleges requires good communication skills because these individuals bring a wide range of experiences and perspectives to the department.

- **If you are an academic dean,** consider using this book as a training guide for all new department chairs.

- **If you are a department chair,** use this book as a guide to improve the effectiveness of your communication in your role as a departmental leader, a manager, a coach, and a mentor.

This book was developed based on training that I provided at Academic Impressions' 2014 conference for department chairs. Each chapter is focused on a specific communication skill (active listening, supportive communication, evaluating and responding effectively to faculty complaints, etc.), and each chapter offers practical tips and examples, an illustrative scenario, and a communication strategies toolbox to help you develop each skill.

Though rendered anonymous, the illustrative scenarios are based on actual situations that chairs have faced in the past. Sharing genuine experiences with chairs will demonstrate how to develop and use these skills. This is not to imply that the specific suggestions herein will work in every situation that appears to be similar, but the hope is that these accounts of past incidents will aid in brainstorming how to apply these communication skills in practice, in your own work.

SKILL #1: ACTIVE LISTENING

Where Chairs Can Go Wrong

Effective communication with colleagues will make—or break—a department chair. Even a chair who excels at other critical job functions (such as fundraising) may be considered unsuccessful by the dean and the faculty if that chair is unable to deal effectively with disgruntled departmental citizens. I often hear comments from deans such as: "Joe is a great fundraiser, but his faculty hate him, so I don't know how much longer I can leave him in the chair's position."

The two most common reasons that chairs are removed from their positions are:

- Their dean receives consistent complaints from faculty and/or students about the chair's inability to address their problems.

- The faculty feel that the chair is unresponsive to their needs and, as a result, are uncooperative at best or, at worst, are openly antagonistic to the chair.

How does this happen? Frequently, these issues develop when chairs ignore long-standing faculty complaints, avoid communicating with "difficult" personalities, or sidestep unpleasant situations because a solution is not clear or obvious.

A Communication Strategies Toolbox

As a department chair, one cannot govern in a top-down mode, but rather must work cooperatively with the faculty. Therefore, a toolbox of communication strategies is needed that will help address problems even with the most difficult of individuals. Several years ago, a successful chair shared that he believed the secret to his success was listening first in any discussion or argument in which he was involved. **Active listening** is a critical part of the department chair's skill set.

In the pages that follow are strategies and sample scenarios to help build a toolbox of active listening strategies. This will review practical tips for:

1. Taking a step back to learn more and to avoid making quick decisions with only partial information.

2. Asking "encouraging questions" to uncover what is really at stake for your colleague.

3. Using "patient listening" to manage difficult people and complex complaints and conflicts.

4. Communicating in ways that will help you make the right decision in new or unfamiliar situations.

I. Step Back and Learn More before Choosing Your Response

Active listening can help you avoid making hasty decisions based on limited information in order to cope with urgent problems that appear to need immediate and decisive action.

It's always critical to step back and learn more.

Practical Tips

To engage in active listening:

Elements of Active Listening	
Pay attention	Maintain comfortable eye contact and nod your head to signal you understand and are listening. These behaviors demonstrate that you are paying attention and can help the speaker calm down and relax
Ask encouraging questions and/or repeat points back	Do this to help the speaker clarify unclear points; this conveys that you understand the problem or complaint.
Be patient	Don't rush the speaker or ask them to "jump to the end." If the speaker feels rushed, they may skip important context
Take notes and summarize the speaker's points at the end	This helps in remembering important points and allows you the opportunity to ensure that you understand their perspective on the situation

Scenario

A colleague was in the first month of his new chair position. His first few weeks were fraught with the stress of beginning a new fall term as complaints abounded: students needed to drop and add courses, new faculty had many questions, and many of them were unfamiliar with university processes. Also, the chair was experiencing anxiety; he felt that the faculty and staff were judging his performance on a daily basis so he wanted to appear decisive.

Late one day, one of his program directors, Sheila, came to him upset. She began with, "We've got a huge problem that we must deal with immediately. I think we need to call Bob in and reprimand him today! He is lying to our students."

Her sense of urgency was infectious and encouraged the chair to act quickly before he fully understood the situation. He picked up his phone and called Bob, a seasoned department academic advisor, into his office and allowed Shelia to passionately accuse Bob of undermining her authority by telling students that she was unresponsive to his requests for her to add an additional section of the Foundations course.

Bob reacted defensively and repeatedly denied the accusation. Realizing that both parties were becoming increasingly angry, the chair ended the meeting by saying that he would "deal with the problem tomorrow."

But Shelia and Bob merely took their disagreement out of his office and continued to argue in an escalating manner. The long-term results were severe bad feelings between Shelia and Bob that drove Bob to apply for another position on campus, where he was hired. Thus, the department lost an experienced academic advisor.

The disagreement between Bob and Shelia was a misunderstanding. Bob had not tried to undermine Shelia's authority, but she had received incorrect information from a poorly informed student that made her feel angry and defensive. Her outrage was not unwarranted, but the chair's decision to call Bob in for a meeting with her at that time was not the best way to handle the situation. Unfortunately, the argument that ensued was more serious than the situation merited, and Bob left the department even after the disagreement was resolved.

If the chair had used active listening skills to take control of the situation, rather than calling Bob in while Shelia was still feeling angry and defensive, he may have avoided much of the negative behavior that occurred.

After this experience, I counseled my colleague to employ active listening when faced with a situation that, at least at first, appears to call for a quick solution. Active listening allows the chair to take control of the communication situation, and to fully understand while simultaneously conveying that he/she cares about the issue and the feelings of the individuals involved. This combination can lower the anxiety or anger of the participants while giving the chair what he/she needs to make a good decision in a prompt, but not rash, manner. Active listening is the key to deescalating a situation, while also gathering information to effectively address the problem.

Practical Tip for Dealing with Schedule Constraints

Department chairs have limited time and busy schedules. A chair might run out of scheduled time before an active listening session has successfully concluded. Don't worry about the time. In the vast majority of cases, the colleague or student will understand and accept that you have a busy schedule and that you must end the conversation temporarily.

The best way to handle this type of situation is to be honest and say, "I'm very sorry we're out of time, but I want to hear more about this problem. Can you come back later today or tomorrow?" If you are not able to meet face-to-face, suggest a follow-up phone call. The important point is not to worry about completing a conversation in a predetermined amount of time. You don't have to wrap up and resolve every problem or concern within a specific meeting timeframe. Spending a little extra time later may be well worth the wait, as you'll have more information in the long run. Additionally, the time in between the two sessions allows you to think about the issue and perhaps develop helpful questions for the second session. It also gives your colleague or student an opportunity to mull it over and to approach the next conversation with some good ideas about how to move forward.

II. Ask Encouraging Questions to Uncover What Is Really at Stake

Often, a colleague will focus on the facts of a situation when telling you about it. Although these facts are important, very often they do not reveal what is really at stake for your colleague from an emotional perspective. More than likely, the real problem goes deeper and your colleague may feel that he/she is not being respected or that his/her opinions are not valued.

Examples

- "How did you interpret her remark?"

- "Why do you think he behaved that way?"

- "What do you think would have been the proper action in that case?"

- "How did that action/remark make you feel?"

- "Have you had similar experiences like this in the past?"

- "What response has worked well for you in the past?"

- "How would you handle this, if you were me?"

Scenario

A junior faculty member, Jean, approached me and she was very upset. She was passionately complaining about a contentious discussion with a colleague, Dwight. In the course of the discussion, I briefly repeated a point back to her with clarifying language:

"So his visit to your office today, Jean, was about his desire to teach the required research methods course that you are scheduled to teach next term. Is that right? And this is the first time you were made aware of Dwight's interest in teaching the course?"

That final sentence is a question phrased as a clarifying statement. Repeating the point showed her explanation was understood, and the additional clarifying language prompted further elaboration on the point. Knowing if this was an ongoing concern between these colleagues or a single incident was important.

In this case, it was a single incident and I soon learned that Dwight felt that he needed to teach the required course so that he could recruit lab assistants from the students in the course. As a solution, Jean invited Dwight to guest lecture for a couple of class meetings to speak about his research and express an interest in recruiting students from the course.

III. Use Patient Listening to Manage Difficult People

If colleagues can share their concerns and feelings—and know that you are listening actively—the tension can significantly lessen. They will be more able to engage collaboratively with you and others in the department to solve problems and achieve goals.

It's surprising how often a colleague shares long, complex stories about why they are disgruntled, only to end with, "Thank you for listening. I realize there's not anything you can do to fix this situation, but I certainly feel better having told you about it."

So be patient and let your colleagues speak their minds. That act alone will make it easier for them to put their anger, anxiety, or mistrust aside and engage more positively.

Scenario

A staff member, Carol, was angry about having to answer the phone for a junior faculty member, Roger, who refused to use voicemail for his messages. Carol felt that Roger was being unreasonable and forcing her to do work that was beneath her position. After speaking with her, I realized that she routinely answered phones for several faculty in the department without concern, but for some reason resented doing it for Roger. In an active listening session, Carol confided in me that she felt like Roger did not appreciate her work and that he was an unreasonably difficult person to work with. In my experience, Roger was labeled a difficult person because his communication behavior radiated an "I'm smarter and more important that you" attitude that many of his colleagues and departmental staff found infuriating and rude.

In this case, I used active listening and met with Roger in his office for more than an hour one afternoon when the department was quieter than usual. After talking with Roger, I realized that Carol, who was older, intimidated him and he felt like she took issue with everything he said. In his frustration, his communication behavior only reinforced Carol's negative perception of Roger and the result was that the more they communicated, the more their relationship worsened. This fact is essential to the problem because when Carol was forced to take phone messages for Roger, she was then forced to communicate with him about the messages. Thus, a task that she performed for others without incident was an anxiety-producing endeavor for her because she didn't want to communicate with Roger.

After an active listening session with Roger, I understood that Roger was intimidated by Carol because she had been in the department for many years and was well liked by the senior faculty, and he felt that she viewed him as an outsider, and responded negatively to his requests in a way that he believed was disrespectful. Roger agreed that I understood his perspective, and felt that I listened carefully and cared about his concerns. The result of our active listening meeting was that he was very willing to engage in a subsequently facilitated meeting with Carol when I asked.

In the end, I was able to have a session with both Carol and Roger in which they both felt safe expressing their feelings and were able to restore collegial relations and move forward in a healthy working relationship.

By being willing to listen to their perspectives, I understood that the stated problem (Roger was unreasonably requiring Carol to answer his phone) was merely a symptom of a relationship misunderstanding in which Roger was intimidated by the older Carol, and believed she was disrespectful of his position. Once they were professionally reconciled, they were able to avoid further problems and disagreements.

Discussion

Usually, we regard colleagues as "difficult people" when we find it difficult to communicate with them. These colleagues may engage in:

- Bullying language

- Overly defensive language

- Rudeness, such as frequently cutting others off, using language to belittle or dismiss others, using nonverbal cues to indicate dislike or disinterest (e.g. rolling their eyes); and/or

- Refusing to engage by "storming off" or accusing others of attacking them.

This is why communication strategies are key to helping chairs deal with these individuals more effectively. I am often told that I am "good with difficult people." My secret weapon is active listening. Surprisingly often, difficult people are difficult because they feel that no one is listening to them. By practicing active listening, you give them what they want the most: the chance to be heard and understood.

Listening to the speaker's perspective means working hard to hear and understand the problem from his/her point of view. There is wisdom in the old adage that there is much to learn by walking in someone else's shoes—or at least trying to imagine what that walk is like. Attempting to understand the problem from the speaker's perspective does not mean you must agree with his/her interpretation. Agreement isn't necessary to be empathetic and supportive. However, making an effort to understand a situation from his/her perspective will help you address it from an empathetic position.

To accomplish this, start by opening your mind and setting aside any preconceived ideas or impressions that you have about the person or the situation, and then embrace the speaker's view as you listen. Even if you are convinced that the speaker's viewpoint is wrong, set that notion aside and hear what the speaker is saying as if you were in his/her shoes. Again, you don't have to agree with him/her in order to listen with an open mind. Without an open mind, you are wasting the time of both parties since you may have already decided that the speaker is wrong and you will not benefit from hearing his/her perspective.

Understanding your colleague's view may offer insight that leads to a solution that satisfies his/her needs. And that provides you a powerful opportunity—because if you can solve the problem now, perhaps you can avoid similar issues in the future.

IV. Finding the Right Decision When You're New to the Process

Academic administrators, especially department chairs early in their careers, often find themselves presented with challenges or problems in unfamiliar areas in which they have little experience, such as budget crises, research grant problems, scientific misconduct charges, or student discipline issues. In these situations and others, chairs must quickly learn about a new task or process. This type of on-the-job learning is challenging and fraught with opportunities for mistakes and unintended consequences. By applying active listening skills, the chair can benefit by learning about the situation while working toward a satisfactory course of action.

Scenario

Last year, a chair contacted me for help with a complaint from a graduate student who felt that her major professor had committed scientific misconduct. It was a serious claim, as the student believed the faculty member had used her research data and presented it as his data. As you likely know, a scientific misconduct investigation is a very formal process and unfamiliar to most faculty and chairs since most chairs never see a case of scientific misconduct in their departments. In this case, the chair was surprised by the claim, as the accused faculty member was a well-respected researcher with a long, successful history of federal agency support and high impact publications. Therefore, she was also understandably skeptical and wanted to protect the professor from what she feared was a mistaken claim.

As we worked through the formal process together, I also coached her on using active listening to discuss the situation with both the student and the faculty member so she could hear the facts from each perspective. After several successful active listening sessions, she was able to understand the situation from both sides. In this case, the faculty member's perspective was that the student was doing research in his funded lab and was being supported by his funded grants, so therefore, the data was his. The student's perspective was that she had designed and run the experiment and thus the data was hers. In the end, the chair was able to reach a formal agreement between the two in which both were able to use the data with proper attribution and written permissions.

Summary

Active listening is an effective communication skill that can benefit department chairs in a wide range of interactions—from the collegial to the adversarial. This skill can be employed either in one-on-one meetings or in larger meetings where you need to facilitate a discussion with opposing parties present. Given that department chairs need to be able to deal with a wide range of issues (from student complaints to faculty disagreements) and constituents (students, faculty, staff, and alumni), active listening is a versatile tool that helps academic administrators negotiate diverse points of view and potentially charged feelings in the room. Active listening can also help chairs navigate difficult and challenging situations in which they have little or no training.

Department chairs must be leaders, managers, mentors, and coaches in their daily professional lives and have often received too little formal training for all of these roles. When combined with the fact that they do not have the full repertoire of incentives and sanctions that are available to managers outside of academia, the need for chairs to have more training in how to motivate their departmental citizens to work collaboratively and to be supportive of goals and initiatives is essential.

A long-term successful chair told me once, "You will never successfully make anyone do anything in an academic department that will be a true win for the department. The only way to move the department forward is to garner the buy-in of the departmental goals and vision."

By practicing active listening, you can get a better sense of the scope of a problem and hopefully find the best way forward. Active listening is a key strategy to help you manage effectively so that you can lead successfully.

SKILL #2: SUPPORTIVE COMMUNICATION

Where Chairs Can Go Wrong

As you know, chairs garner support by building strong working connections with their departmental colleagues and staff. Strong professional relationships provide a solid foundation for collaboration with staff and faculty to accomplish strategic goals and maintain a smoother operation. Unfortunately, after months or years on the job, the stressful demands of the position can lead to communication behaviors that can damage collegial relations or even, in the worst cases, cause resentment, distrust, and hurt feelings.

Two common problems that once successful chairs face are:

- Loss of support from faculty and staff

- Allowing their communication styles to become non-supportive

These two problems are often closely related and worsen over time as the pressures of the job take a toll on a chair's communication choices. In the following sections, I will address each of these challenges and discuss how supportive communication strategies can help.

A Communication Strategies Toolbox

Supportive communication strategies are a significant part of a chair's repertoire because they help build healthy professional relationships and aid the chair in avoiding common challenges they may face.

Supportive Communication Strategies:

1. Avoid evaluating/judgmental language

2. Focus on problem solving

3. Keep communication lines open

4. Practice empathy

I. Avoid Evaluating/Judgmental Language

Unfortunately, faculty resentment and distrust of a chair is fairly common at some institutions of higher education. However, when these feelings are caused by communication behaviors, they can be effectively addressed and the chair can begin to recreate a supportive environment with his/her faculty. A key communication culprit is the overuse of judgmental language. The use of judgmental language leads to defensiveness because it suggests that the speaker is placing blame on another party. Judgmental language is characterized by words that point out a person's faults and often begin with the word "you."

Examples include:

■   "You don't respect deadlines."

■   "You are stubborn."

■   "You are close-minded."

■   "You don't listen."

In contrast, supportive communication focuses on descriptive language to define problems or complaints. Instead of saying to a faculty member, "You must stop canceling classes," try neutral descriptive language such as, "I've received two complaints from students this week about canceled classes and would like to hear your side of the story." Using descriptive language is less threatening because it focuses on specific instances of behavior and does not feel harshly judgmental or overly critical.

Moreover, using descriptive language can help formulate a positive outcome for communication. For example, if a chair expresses to a faculty member, "Your perspective on the proposed curriculum changes are old-fashioned and you are being stubborn by clinging to them," the faculty member might easily become defensive and feel that he must cling even more fervently to his position (a negative outcome). Using supportive communication, a chair might phrase the statement differently by saying, "I see your point, but can you think of other options that might work equally well?" This invites the faculty member to think beyond his current position and participate in a more positive outcome. The chair builds support for the curriculum changes rather than simply putting the faculty member on the defensive.

The overuse of judgmental language can also cause the faculty to distrust and even resent the chair. This is an unhealthy environment for the chair as he/she needs to maintain a positive working relationship with faculty in order to lead and manage effectively.

Scenario

Recently, I was working with a chair who felt that his faculty colleagues had "abandoned him" and were "working against" him on every initiative. Frankly, he was very surprised since the first three years of his five year term had been quite successful and he felt that he had helped lead the department forward. After reviewing his record with him, I agreed that he had been an effective leader, but that he was losing the support of his faculty. In an effort to help, with his permission, I contacted several of the senior faculty and soon learned that his concerns were valid: he was losing their support. From their perspective, their chair had been a supportive and helpful colleague and leader early in his term and that, in turn, had motivated the faculty to be supportive of his initiatives. However, over the last year or so, they felt that he had developed a negative view of them and increasingly blamed them for departmental problems. As a result, they no longer felt that it was worth their time and effort to help him. When I asked for examples, the faculty consistently cited the chair's communication style as proof of his negative perspective and lack of support for their work and service.

When I asked how his communication style had changed over the years, the faculty pointed out that the chair had become short tempered, rude, and dismissive of their thoughts and ideas. Armed with this information, I worked with the chair to see if we could identify problems and solutions.

What we found is not surprising to anyone who has served as a department chair for several years. Since the demands of the job are so great and the challenges formidable, department chairs must deal with many stressful pressures from many sources, including their departmental constituents and their dean's office. Wedged between the demands of faculty, students, and administrative bosses, department chairs can face position burn out quickly. This condition is exacerbated when the chair doesn't receive training that can help him cope with the ever increasing demands that the position brings.

Over the years, the chair's growing burnout had manifested itself in his communication behaviors. As he became increasingly busy, his patience decreased and his faculty interpreted his lack of patience as having a short temper. They found that he no longer took time to patiently talk with them about their concerns, even though he frequently asked them to help him with problems. They considered this behavior rude. Their experience suggested that the chair was all too eager to tell them how to do things, while being very dismissive of their ideas. And finally, they interpreted his frequent communications about "what the dean thinks" as an indication that he had no interest in their perspectives.

Of course the chair realized that the stress of the position did seem to make him more physically tired and even "a little cross" at times, but he had not realized the extent to which his communication behaviors were damaging his relationship with his faculty and, in turn, his ability to achieve his unit's goals. Once he had this information, he was able to begin rebuilding the support of his faculty through the use of supportive communication strategies.

II. Focus on Problem Solving

Closely related to using descriptive rather than judgmental language is using language that focuses on problem solving. Using problem solving oriented language in conjunction with neutral descriptive language can help chairs address performance in positive ways. Consider a staff member, Reggie, who is habitually late in providing monthly budget reports. Rather than reprimanding him, a chair could use supportive communication techniques to explain the problem in a nonthreatening way and invite him to participate in solving the problem: "I need to receive budget reports on time, but your past three budget reports have arrived at least one week late. Let's talk about how we can help you make those deadlines in the future."

Consider, again, that a chair has received complaints that a senior faculty member, Regina, is being rude to two junior faculty, Patricia and John, when they are interacting at meetings of the curriculum committee. It would be best to have the committee functioning collegially, so a chair might approach Regina and say, "Patricia and John have expressed their concern that you are not giving their suggestions proper consideration. Can you please clarify your position at the next meeting? This is a good opportunity for Patricia and John to learn more about your views."

These examples demonstrate how using descriptive language and focusing on problem solving, rather than criticism, can invite others to participate in positive outcomes and can help individuals engage collegially. Supportive communication focuses on problem solving, not blame, and uses descriptive language to explain a concern with the goal of enlisting the other person's help, rather than putting him/her on the defensive.

III. Keep Communication Lines Open

As a department chair, one has to make decisions, but the way decisions are communicated to colleagues can make a significant difference in how faculty respond to these decisions, and whether or not the chair will receive support. A common communication mistake occurs when chairs announce decisions or changes from an "on high" stance that conveys that they are unilaterally deciding how matters are to be handled. These types of authoritative declarations can cause colleagues to feel undervalued, or can even unnecessarily place colleagues in an adversarial position, if they disagree with the chair's pronouncement. If they feel adversarial, they will be far less likely to support the chair's position and the chair may end up spending more time defending his/her decision, rather than getting on with the work.

Instead of announcing decisions from a supervisory position, a chair can invite colleagues to participate in the decision-making process and offer possible solutions to consider. Ultimately, the chair will choose the solution that he/she thinks is best, or amend one a solution to fit the department's needs. In order to invite feedback, the chair can use an existing committee or form an ad hoc working group to advise him/her. Inviting such committees and groups to seek solutions also allows them to deal with any preexisting concerns that may be attached to the issue. These preexisting concerns are the baggage that makes an issue thornier than its basic nature warrants. Hence, a chair can present a problem to the group and ask for three or four possible solutions. Remember, one can structure advice requests so that they are not binding: "I would like for you all to look at this problem and come up with some recommendations for me to consider. Although I may not be able to follow your advice exactly, I know I'll benefit greatly from your feedback." Inviting colleagues to participate in the decision helps to avoid declarations that may make the chair appear less collegial.

Here are four ways to keep communication open and productive:

- Use active listening to help you hear others and to let them know that they are being heard.

- React positively to other's comments, even if you disagree: "I can see how you feel that way, but can you see my concern?"

- Remind others that they are important to the unit: "Your long service in the department gives you unique insight into many of our challenges."

- Encourage them to express their views and thoughts using questions such as, "What do you suggest is a good resolution?"

Scenario

A chair was recently asked by her dean to put the introductory course for her program's curriculum online so that it would be easier for students to enroll in the course (historically, the course has had long waiting lists). The dean's hope was that offering the course online would remedy the long wait lists for the on-campus course and help students progress more quickly to graduation (improving time to graduation is a university-level strategic goal). But some of her senior faculty have long been suspicious of the academic rigor of online courses, so there was some baggage attached to the dean's request. Since she knew that one of her junior faculty members had some experience with online learning and an interest in developing online courses, she formed a small ad hoc work group that included the junior faculty member along with a key senior faculty member and a representative from the campus teaching and learning center. At the committee's first meeting, she explained how the dean's request was linked to the strategic plan of the University and charged the work group with providing three or four recommendations on how best to implement the dean's request.

The key is that she asked the faculty to share in the responsibility for making this decision for the department. Ultimately, the ad hoc work group came forward with a recommendation to put the course online and the faculty were included in the decision process.

IV. Practice Empathy

Practicing empathy can help you involve colleagues who may feel marginalized or undervalued by demonstrating that you understand their feelings. Most department chairs find many preexisting problems in the unit when they take over as the key administrative officer. There may be a good bit of baggage that comes with certain departmental members based on years of what they may consider mistreatment. Many of these people feel marginalized and undervalued and may have become cranky, obstinate, or consistently negative in their attitudes and language, which is bad for departmental morale. I've heard some administrators refer to these types of individuals as bad faculty, as in, "Professor Smith is just a bad faculty member."

Although I realize that some people will always be more pessimistic than others, I don't embrace the concept of a "Bad Fac". In my experience, many faculty and staff are disgruntled for legitimate reasons. Even if you can't address their specific problems, such as a failed promotion attempt, you can empathize with their feelings. Regardless of the individual's specific issues, many of the communication strategies described in this book can also help you practice empathy, particularly:

- Active listening that shows you are engaged and interested in your colleague's problems.

- Avoiding judgmental language that focuses on objective descriptive language can help your colleague feel less defensive.

In addition, I suggest sharing your feelings about similar experiences to help your colleague feel less isolated. Additionally, offering your colleague help, within reason, can make him feel better about his circumstances. In a recent example, a chair received a request from a faculty member who wanted a fall semester release from teaching to work on his book manuscript. Given the department teaching load, the chair knew she couldn't grant the release; instead she met with the faculty member to talk about his needs and shared with him her difficulty in getting her last book manuscript completed. In the end, she arranged for a part-time graduate teaching assistant to help him with grading in his courses and he was pleased with the result.

By practicing empathy with your colleagues, you can help them feel better about themselves and others, help them engage positively in the life of the department, and encourage them to work with you collaboratively.

Summary

As expressed above, a once successful chair found that after a few years he felt abandoned by his department, while his department felt that he had stopped being supportive. In the end, it was his change in communication strategies that drove the department's feelings of non-support. In essence, he was the same person as before, but he had let the stressful nature of the job alter his communication behaviors and, as a result, his performance suffered from his department's lack of support. In an unfortunate, but predictable turn, the less support he received from his faculty, the more stress he felt in his job, and the more he relied on negative communication strategies. Without learning to see the problem from a communication perspective, he might have never been able to reverse the trend.

The communication strategies in this chapter can help you even if you have an excellent relationship with everyone in your department. These strategies help build and maintain trust and collaboration by helping your colleagues feel that you are interested in their views, value their input, and support them. These supportive communication strategies involve a group of techniques and skills that help academic leaders build positive relationships and collaboration efforts. An academic chair can do precious little on his/her own, so building positive relationships within the unit provides the leader with more options for good collaboration that will help accomplish unit goals and provide smoother operations overall.

SKILL #3: RECEIVING, EVALUATING, AND ACTING ON COMPLAINTS

Where Chairs Can Go Wrong

It is common, especially for fairly new department chairs, to feel overwhelmed with the large number of complaints they receive. A department chair with whom I worked recently said, "Sometimes it feels like all I do is spend every day dealing with complaints."

Three common mistakes chairs make in handling complaints are:

- Not effectively dealing with complaints, thus prompting the complainers to "move up" to the next administrative level

- Spending all of their time dealing with complaints, thus leaving strategic goals and plans to flounder

- Pushing complaints up the to the next administrative level

Dealing with complaints at the unit level is very important for academic chairs because if the complaint remains unresolved in the department, there is a very good chance that the complainer will simply take his problem to the dean's office, the provost's office, or the president's office. In short, complaints seldom, if ever, dissipate on their own, so department chairs must deal with complaints effectively or risk having the complaint escalated to the dean's office.

Since complainers are inclined to take their concerns to the next administrative level if they believe their department chair is not effectively dealing with it, chairs frequently feel pressure to address all complaints immediately. This is admirable, but in doing so, chairs risk spending their whole day addressing one complaint after another as they arise.

The fundamental problem with this approach is that addressing complaints is only part of the chair's work, and if all he/she does is deal with complaints, then the rest of the work goes undone or incomplete, and the department suffers from lack of attention to other, perhaps more important matters. Hence, while department chairs must effectively deal with complaints, they must not allow that duty to dominate their time.

A Communication Strategies Toolbox

Using simple communication strategies for receiving, evaluating, and acting on complaints will help chairs effectively deal with complaints, while lowering the emotional stress related to complaints and providing the chairs with more time to do their other work. The types of complaints that chairs receive most frequently are related to courses, scheduling, budgets, and the like. Issues that involve emergencies, escalating conflicts, or serious disputes that require special and immediate attention are not addressed here.

In this chapter are quick and easy ways to help chairs address the following:

1. Efficiently receiving complaints

2. Effectively evaluating and acting on complaints

I. Efficiently Receiving Complaints

The mode of delivery by which a complaint is received provides chairs with options for how to best deal with each one. Complaints are typically communicated in one of four ways:

- In person (one-on-one or in small groups)

- Via phone

- Via email

- In meetings

Receiving complaints in person

One effective strategy for dealing with complaints that are presented in person is to include regular office hours, drop-in times, or open-door periods in your weekly schedule. These periods are akin to faculty office hours. Schedule such periods late in the day, when faculty and students often have free time in their busy schedules.

Scenario

On your way back from a meeting, you run into Professor Williams, who stops you to complain about the new travel insurance form that the college has recently adopted. You listen for a moment or two and then politely say, "Bob, thanks for bringing that to my attention. Please come by my office during my drop-in time so that we can discuss this more. Your experience can help us improve the form's usability."

Allocating dedicated time in a chair's calendar allows one to quickly schedule complaint time when one is faced with a concern in person. It also helps to establish boundaries so that the chair is able to accomplish all of the important work that needs to be addressed during the day.

Receiving complaints via phone

A busy chair can't spend fifteen to thirty minutes on every phone call; there is not enough time in the day. It is inadvisable to try to resolve complaints with only the information that can be gathered in a quick phone call. Most phone chats are, by their very nature, one-sided in perspective. Moreover, trying to deal with a complaint "cold" (the first time it's presented from a single perspective) in a phone call risks less-informed decision making. That uninformed, or less informed, decision can actually make the problem worse by producing unforeseen consequences.

Scenario

Recently I called Jim, a department chair, with a question about why one of his instructors had not completed some required online IT security training. This instructor, Cameron, was the only full-time employee in the school who had not completed the training. Jim exasperatedly told me that he tried everything he could think of to motivate Cameron to complete the training and didn't know what else he could do.

Without following my own advice, I said, "Tell Cameron that the provost's office expects him to have completed the training by tomorrow afternoon." With that, we ended our call and I felt I had given Jim the help he needed. Alas, within minutes I received a call from the school IT manager, Suzanne, telling me that Cameron had just returned to campus for the training. After a brief conversation, the Suzanne told me that she would address the issue, and Cameron finished the training by the end of the day. Reflecting on my mistake, I concluded that instead of just speaking with Jim, I should have asked him to have Suzanne give me a call so that I could get a fuller understanding of the situation.

Take two steps

I recommend a two-step process when receiving complaints by phone. First, I ask the caller for a brief overview of the complaint so I can evaluate the problem. Think of this step as conducting triage (determining the seriousness or urgency of the complaint). Second, once I have an idea of the gravity of the complaint, I can usually address it in one of three ways:

- I ask the person to send me an email with the details of the complaint and some suggestions for possible resolutions. I find that the complainer often has given the issue a great amount of thought and will have some good solutions in mind.

- Delegate the complaint to someone who is in a better position to resolve the situation successfully. For example, when it comes to a complaint about a student's class schedule, the student's academic advisor is much better informed than a department chair and has the necessary information and experience to deal with that complaint.

- Similar to open-door drop-in times, I schedule time in my week to return phone calls. That way when I receive a complaint by phone, I can easily schedule a callback time by saying, "I'd like to call you back today at 3:00 pm. Will that work for you?"

Receiving complaints via email

Emails are essential to the academic unit's ability to function efficiently, but too often academic leaders complain that they have to devote too much time to a constant flood of emails. However, just as in dealing with phone calls, there are helpful ways to deal with complaints received via email. The first is to schedule time each day to respond to emails. Don't respond to complaints the moment you receive them, unless they are urgent and you believe they can be quickly resolved. I encourage you to schedule email response time for later in the day and save your morning hours to deal with other matters.

During scheduled email time, respond to each email, even if it's only to say that you need more time to properly respond, so that the sender doesn't feel ignored. During the morning, students and faculty are heavily involved in their class work, so there are fewer interruptions then. Given that situation, one may find success in using the morning hours for work that requires focused concentration time, such as writing and research.

I prefer to save the late afternoon hours for open office hours and returning phone calls and emails. Of course, departmental cultures and contexts may be quite different among themselves, so you should do what is best for your own situation. The goal is to closely protect some quiet work time in your schedule every day in order to make progress on your top initiatives or projects.

One advantage to receiving complaints via email is that they are easily delegated to others who are better situated to handle the complaint (advisors, program leaders, committee chairs, etc.). By simply forwarding the email to the appropriate person and copying the original sender, you can appropriately delegate the complaint and let the sender know you have done so.

For example, in response to a complaint about the department's guidelines for the tenure and promotion process, you could forward the email to the chair of the Promotion and Tenure Committee and copy the sender: "Crystal, as chair of the Promotion and Tenure Committee, please respond to Andrea's email (I've copied Andrea here)." Immediately forwarding the complaint to someone who can best deal with the specific concern is much quicker and more efficient than offering an opinion while suggesting that the sender follow up with the appropriate person.

Receiving complaints in meetings

With that said, regular meetings that are designed to allow stakeholders to present their concerns are fundamental to effectively managing complaints. Monthly meetings with student leaders, staff members, and key faculty committees provide structured time for open dialogue, building positive relationships, and providing a valuable mechanism for receiving complaints.

For example, you may schedule a monthly meeting with your departmental student leaders where everyone knows that the purpose of the meeting is for the leaders to present concerns from students and to hear about any you may have. It's essential for all participants to understand that their issues might not be resolved during the meeting, as the point of the meeting is simply to present the issues. Such meetings can be helpful because they channel complaints to the meeting, rather than having all complaints come from individuals via a less structured process. In this model, the stakeholders themselves help the process by eliminating complaints they deem to have less importance.

In order for such meetings to be optimally effective, the agendas should be set by the stakeholders and sent to you in advance for your review. The advance notice allows you to review the agenda and invite others to attend who are well suited to address the concerns, such as your senior student advisor or your departmental IT manager.

Additionally, if there is an agenda item that is not appropriate for the meeting (for instance, a complaint about the departmental receptionist), you can head that off and explain that this particular meeting is not the proper venue for handling such an issue and arrange another way, such as a private meeting with you, to hear that concern. This way you'll save much more time than you would have to spend if you dealt with each individual complaint that may come to you on an ad hoc basis.

These regularly scheduled meetings also provide a venue for dealing with complaints that you receive in person, by phone, and through email, as you can defer them by asking that they be placed on the agenda of an upcoming meeting. For example, conducting regularly scheduled meetings with important committees, such as the departmental Curriculum Committee or the Promotion and Tenure Committee, provides you with a venue to address specific concerns related to the charges of the committees.

Scenario

One of your faculty members comes to you with a concern about proposed changes in the required research methods course. Rather than trying to address her concern on your own, it's probably more efficient to ask that her concern be placed on the next agenda for the Curriculum Committee. Relatedly, deferring complaints to meetings can also help you avoid inadvertently causing a rift between yourself and one of your committee chairs.

For instance, not long ago I worked with a department chair, Annette, who unwittingly angered one of her program chairs, Frank, by consistently dealing with complaints about the program without including Frank or the program's steering committee. Although Annette thought she was being helpful, Frank felt his authority was being undermined and was ready to step down as program chair. Annette's actions mistakenly made her appear to be micromanaging the committee's responsibilities, which is a bad situation for an administrator who relies on the support of her colleagues.

II. Evaluating and Acting on Complaints

Dealing with complaints without a strategy can prevent you from doing your job effectively and diminish your morale as you become overwhelmed with what seems to be an endless flow of complaints. A key to effectively dealing with complaints is to determine their seriousness or urgency early on so that you don't spend time on a complaint that should be delegated when you have a more urgent complaint awaiting your attention. Highly urgent or serious complaints must be handled quickly, but most complaints can be handled effectively by using a communication strategy that fits your unit's culture and provides you with time to do all of your work.

Effectively dealing with complaints is a two-step process of evaluating and acting on the complaints. Evaluating is a type of triage, determining the urgency or seriousness of the complaint. Acting is determining when and how to deal with the complaint. I find that one simple chart demonstrates this process well:

Triage: Urgency and Seriousness Level	Action: When and How
Low level Examples: • Student complaint about future course offerings • Faculty complaint about need to upgrade to the latest Word processing software version • Staff complaint about student workers being late to work	Delegate, if possible. Otherwise, save for a later scheduled time (email time or meetings).
Mid-level Examples: • Student grade complaint • Faculty complaint about students being late for her class • Staff complaint about coworker taking a long lunch hour.	Delegate, if appropriate. Otherwise, deal with it during office hours or email time.
High level Examples: • Parent complaint about his student being bullied in the lab • Faculty complaint about students cheating in class • Staff complaint about financial misconduct by a coworker	Delegate, if appropriate. Otherwise, deal with it before the end of the day.

The chart prompts the user to determine the urgency or seriousness of the complaint first and then look at the suggested action. If you triage a complaint to have a low level in terms of urgency or seriousness, the first option under "Action" is to delegate the complaint. Although learning to delegate is essential for an academic chair, it's sometimes a difficult skill to use because the chair may not want to bother others with complaints, or he/she may be anxious about relying on others to handle the complaint effectively.

Delegating is an important skill to develop in its own right, but for the sake of this discussion, know that there are other departmental members such as advisors, staff, and faculty who are better informed to deal with many of the complaints that come to your office.

However, if delegating is not an option for you, save the complaint to be addressed during a later scheduled time. The context surrounding each complaint is important in determining its triage level, but in most cases, a student complaint about the course schedule for the upcoming term will be considered a low-level complaint that should be delegated to your top academic advisor.

Note also that the first option in the mid-level triage row is also to delegate the complaint, if it's appropriate to do so. In such cases, it may be the context of the complaint that raises it above the lowest level because of its urgency or seriousness. Returning to the example of a student complaint about class scheduling for the upcoming term, the seriousness or urgency level might increase if you know that the student is on track to graduate in the next term and that her problem is shared by numerous other seniors, all of whom may not be able to graduate unless an accommodation can be found. This context raises the urgency level of the complaint, but does not necessarily negate the need to delegate it to your top academic advisor. However, in this case, you can ask the advisor to look into the situation immediately and report back to you as soon as possible with his ideas for a solution.

Highly urgent complaints and emergencies must be handled quickly, but most complaints can still be handled effectively by using a communication strategy that fits your department's culture and provides you with time to do all of your work. Even high-level complaints can be delegated, but you must have a corresponding level of confidence and trust in the person to whom you assign the complaint.

Consequently, explain to that person that you consider this complaint important and that you need him/her to deal with it immediately and effectively. In a case like this, you may ask him/her to get back to you with her plan for resolving the complaint within a specified amount of time so you can approve or amend her plan.

Don't Push Complaints up the Administrative Hierarchy

Most complaints are best resolved at the departmental level. Escalating a complaint occurs when a chair ignores the responsibility to deal with a complaint and simply tells the complainer to take it to the next level of the administrative chain, which is usually the dean's office. This is not an appropriate strategy for addressing most complaints, and it creates at least two problems. First, it may lead to the complainer being passed around from administrator to administrator without having the complaint addressed.

Consider again the student complaint about class scheduling for the next term. I was recently involved in a complaint where the department chair simply told the student, Deborah, to take her complaint to the dean's office. Deborah did so and was properly directed to the associate dean for Academic Affairs. The associate dean appropriately delegated the complaint to the college's top academic advisor. The college's academic advisor evaluated the complaint, rightly decided that it was a department-level complaint, and directed Deborah back to the department chair.

At this point Deborah was angrier about being handed off three times than she was about her initial complaint, and she promptly contacted the president's office with a new complaint: that no one in the department or college would appropriately deal with her problem. At that point, one complaint had grown to two, and the provost's office had to step in and deal with both.

The second issue created is that it makes the chair and his department appear as though they are unwilling to address complaints appropriately. Unfortunately, senior administrators often complain about department chairs who repeatedly push their problems up, and therefore develop a reputation for being poor administrators.

Pushing a complaint up the administrative hierarchy is seldom the appropriate action, as most complaints are best resolved at the departmental level. Whenever a chair needs upper administrative help or advice, it should be sought directly with the appropriate administrator.

Summary

Dealing with complaints without a strategy can waste your time and energy and keep you from doing your job effectively. Managing the time that you handle complaints and planning periods in your schedule for doing so will help you balance the amount of time you spend on complaints with all other responsibilities. Furthermore, using even the simple Triage-Action chart presented above can help you avoid taking on complaints that should be delegated to more appropriate people in the department.

SKILL #4: BUILDING RAPPORT

Where Chairs Can Go Wrong

The concept of academic chair rapport refers to a condition in which the administrator enjoys a positive, supportive relationship with the department's faculty, staff, alumni, and students. This harmony allows chairs to be more effective in their work by providing a collegial, collaborative, and understanding work environment. Because of the goodwill it engenders, building a healthy rapport with your stakeholders is a worthwhile goal and will help you to better manage and lead your unit.

Three serious problems that chairs can face once they've lost a positive rapport with their stakeholders are:

- Decreased effectiveness

- Challenges to authority

- Having their reputation undermined by colleagues

Chairs who do not pay close attention to maintaining a good rapport with their department stakeholders can eventually find themselves in serious situations, such as having their faculty issue a vote of no confidence as leverage with the dean to the have the chair removed.

Scenario

Jean was a new chair hired in a national search into a department that had suffered for many years because the chair did not set departmental goals. The college's dean told Jean that he was counting on her to improve the department's research through increased grants and contract funding. Jean accepted the task with great enthusiasm, but immediately assumed that she knew what was best, and that the department faculty were complacent and unwilling to improve. Acting on her assumptions, Jean established a top-down leadership style and decided which faculty could be productive and which faculty needed to retire to free-up faculty lines for new hires. Due to her actions, the faculty mistrusted Jean, and felt that she was biased and shortsighted. Within 18 months, she had lost the support of all the faculty (including the faculty she considered productive) and a unanimous vote of no confidence gave the dean only one choice. Jean was removed as chair.

A Communication Strategies Toolbox

Building and maintaining a healthy rapport can help the chair avoid serious leadership challenges, as well as help him/her become more effective in achieving departmental and college goals.

Building a good rapport in your department involves the following key strategies:

1. Creating an environment of trust

2. Assuring that stakeholders know their thoughts and feelings are important

3. Being impartial

4. Being open to alternatives

Scenario

A long-term senior faculty member, Bret, emotionally opposed an undergraduate major program closure that the junior faculty members enthusiastically supported. One reason for Bret's opposition was that he fondly remembered the program when it was vibrant and viable, while the newer faculty had no fervent ties to the program. In a department-wide meeting, I encouraged Bret to speak his mind, and he spoke emotionally about his pride in the program and recounted its achievements before it became unattractive to students and its enrollment plummeted. During the meeting, we all listened patiently to Bret and told him that his feelings were important to us. Ultimately, by honoring Bret's feelings, he accepted and supported a well-constructed plan for discontinuing the program.

I. Creating an Environment of Trust

Creating an environment of trust is about helping your constituents feel safe expressing their ideas, thoughts, and perspectives, without fear of retaliation or being held to past statements if they decide to amend their positions. There are several simple steps you can take to help achieve this goal.

Make your office a safe place for the expression of thoughts and feelings

An excellent place to start creating an environment of trust is in your office. Make your office a safe place for individuals to express their ideas and perspectives, even to the point of telling them directly, "This is a safe place. I am not going to breach your confidentiality. I want you to be able to say what you feel you need to say." Since chairs often deal with emotionally charged issues, visitors can become emotional, and those feelings may manifest in communication behaviors that express sadness, anger, and/or resentment. They may raise their voices and use emphatic nonverbal actions, like waving their arms or pounding the table when making a point, at other times, they may cry. When this occurs, I address the behavior by helping the person to understand that it is ok to express these feelings, but for me to deal with their complaints effectively, I need for them to calm down. By establishing your office as a safe place for your departmental citizens to speak frankly, you build their trust by showing them that you are interested in hearing their concerns and aren't trying to find fault or affix blame.

Invite input before making decisions

Although some problems and challenges require immediate decisions, most academic decisions allow time to consider a number of possible solutions before agreeing on a final resolution. Therefore, I encourage chairs to offer their stakeholders time to review and comment on draft proposals and decisions prior to the chair's commitment to a resolution. Of course, it would be impractical to provide every departmental stakeholder the opportunity to comment on every matter, but the chair can build a great deal of goodwill and rapport by sensibly inviting input on important decisions. There are a variety of possible venues for the chair to use, and I encourage chairs to employ as many different options as is reasonable in their departments. Some decisions are best vetted by a senior-level steering committee, often known as an executive committee. These groups typically include representation from the major stakeholders, and are familiar with the details of the department's operations, strengths, areas of needed improvement, and challenges. As a result, such groups are prepared to comment and offer well-informed feedback quickly. Additionally, they can advise the chair to open up certain issues to broader feedback, if they deem it necessary. Executive committees frequently deal with issues related to budgets, hiring, evaluations, alumni relations, and administrative assignments.

When broader feedback is needed, the chair can consider various venues for discussion, including open forums and full departmental meetings. It's always crucial to keep your departmental culture in mind when deciding on venues. If you have a small department where the culture is about garnering consensus, then you need to include as many departmental members as possible. In general, however, I don't recommend bringing every proposal or draft idea to a required meeting of the whole department. Doing so can make required departmental meetings excessively long and tiresome for the stakeholders who don't want to participate in every decision. In short, invite input from the most appropriate stakeholders via the most appropriate venues before committing to a decision or a plan, but don't overburden the departmental members by forcing them to participate in every decision regardless of their interest.

Ultimately the chair will make the final decision, but allowing the appropriate stakeholders to weigh in on the decision before it is finalized will help establish good rapport. The feedback that is received will give the chair a fuller understanding of how the decision will affect the department, provide explicit support from some stakeholders, offer the opportunity to meet with stakeholders who oppose the solution, and offer the chance to back away from an unpopular decision if there is a lack of support. Although this process takes longer than making unilateral decisions, it helps the chair make the best decision for the department, while building departmental rapport.

II. Assuring that Stakeholders Know Their Feelings Are Important

Departmental stakeholders care about their unit and want it to be successful. As a result, they have thoughts and feelings about departmental issues that are important to them both as individuals and as members of the whole. It's impossible for a chair to succeed in leading a department without upsetting some individuals, but one way to ameliorate the negative feelings associated with a decision is ensure that stakeholders know that their thoughts and feelings are important, even when you are unable to do what they prefer.

One effective way to accomplish this is to listen to their feelings and their words. As you do, you can better understand their perspectives, allowing you to appropriately follow up on their concerns. Here are a few examples of good follow-up questions that might help you to better understand your colleagues' feelings:

■   How do you see this decision affecting you personally?

■   What is your biggest concern related to this change?

■   What could we do to lower your concern about this implementation?

By posing these types of questions and carefully listening to the responses, you may be able to separate the emotions related to the issue from the stakeholder's more fundamental concerns. Keep in mind that you don't have to agree with their feelings in order to empathize, but the fact that you take the time to understand their concerns and their feelings will be appreciated and can help strengthen your relationship.

III. Being Impartial

Department members want to feel that the chair's decisions are impartial, evenhanded, and unbiased toward individuals, programs, or groups. In many troubled departments, a fundamental concern of the stakeholders is that the chair is guilty of cronyism, or unfairly favoring one or more people or programs above others. When your stakeholders believe that you are providing them with an equal, unbiased playing field where they can succeed and compete for resources, they will be more willing to get on board with your initiatives, and be more collaborative because they do not see resource allocation as unfair.

A key way to demonstrate impartiality is to develop standardized, objective processes for determining the allocation of resources such as leave time, course assignments, graduate teaching assistant assignments, and work schedules, and then honor those processes. As with many of the topics discussed, you must remain honest to your departmental culture, but I find that unit bylaws are an excellent way to codify processes for determining resource allocations (and reallocations). Therefore, I encourage you to review your departmental bylaws, and if you see opportunities for improvement that will help you allocate resources, appoint a work group to draft a revision of the bylaws to recommend to the department.

Resource allocation often results in winners and losers, and it's the chair's job to notify both. Keep in mind that the perceived "losers" will see this notification as bad news. Like most human beings, chairs don't enjoy delivering bad news, especially if they expect the news to hurt their colleagues' feelings. However, it's better to tell the complete story, in the most positive manner possible, than to shield someone's feelings. When delivering bad news, use these three strategies:

- Be timely: communicating in person is best, but if it must be done by phone in order to make sure that you reach him/her first, then call.

- Be complete: make certain that you know all the details before you start the conversation. Your colleague or student will undoubtedly have questions, and you need to answer his questions without saying "I don't know" or "Let me get back to you on that."

- Be empathetic: maintain a respectful and empathetic demeanor until your colleague or student changes the tone of the conversation.

IV. Being Open to Alternatives

It's normal for us to feel that our answers to problems are the best answers -- otherwise we wouldn't have decided them in the first place. Hence, it's easy to understand that our stakeholders feel the same way about their solutions. Therefore, we should not expect them to always accept our solutions as the best. With this in mind, be open to hearing their thoughts on alternative resolutions. I encourage you to even ask them what alternatives they might see, particularly if they envision a resolution that is better for everyone involved.

Remaining open to alternatives involves investigating all the reasonable alternatives suggested to you. Only by looking into the alternatives can you truly gauge their appropriateness. If the alternatives turn out not to be viable, you'll be able to explain why because you spent time investigating each one.

Scenario

Bob was a faculty member who found himself under pressure from his publisher on a deadline for his book manuscript. Bob asked his chair for a release from teaching in the spring semester so he could focus entirely on the book. Although the chair thought the request was unreasonable, given the department's need for all faculty to teach their required loads, she investigated the viability of Bob's request and found that Bob's leave just wouldn't work for the department. When she met with Bob, she explained, "Bob, I appreciate the deadline pressure that you are feeling, but because of our decreased funding and loss of a part-time instructor, I'm unable to give you a release from teaching in the spring." Although this was not the answer that Bob had hoped for, the chair was able to demonstrate to Bob that she had investigated his request and gave him concrete reasons for why she was unable to grant his request.

Bob understood the situation and accepted that she could not give him a release from teaching so he asked her for a graduate teaching assistant (GTA) to help with his grading load in his spring courses. Once she investigated this alternative, she found that she could accommodate this request and was able to agree with Bob on his workable solution. By remaining open to alternatives, the chair was able to help Bob with his deadline pressures and reinforced Bob's opinion that she is fair and open minded.

Summary

Using the discussed strategies to build rapport in your department can help you to deliver bad news more easily, create a collaborative collegial environment that can facilitate success, and develop your reputation as a fair administrator. When you have established good rapport and are known to be fair, you'll find that others want to help you succeed as chair.

SKILL #5: IMPROVING PROBLEM SOLVING

Where Chairs Can Go Wrong

Academic departments experience many challenges each year that require thoughtful problem solving, however, most academic problems can be solved through a variety of methods.   Finding the most appropriate method can help the chair avoid unforeseen difficulties that result from stakeholder misunderstandings or misperceptions. One solution might be slightly less expensive than another or one more time consuming, but overall, expense and time-to-solution are not always the best criteria. Other considerations may include department culture, values, history, and/or the need to mesh with a college or university strategic plan. A chair who looks for the quickest route to a solution may actually derail the process by cutting short the time that would allow faculty get comfortable with plan and, therefore, support the plan.

Common problems associated with flawed plans that can lead to an inability to successfully implement are:

- Misdiagnosing the problem

- Not allowing for a careful review and feedback on a proposed solution

- A solution focused on the symptoms rather than the source of the problem

Establishing a thoughtful process to facilitate decision making will help you avoid counter-productive actions.

A Communication Strategies Toolbox

The following five strategies are designed to help chairs improve their department's problem-solving processes:

1. Agreeing on the problem

2. Involving the affected people in the solution

3. Agreeing to a plan

4. Carefully vetting the agreed-upon solution

5. Publicizing the implementation

Incorporating these five strategies into your department's problem-solving processes will help find solutions that are well-conceived and supported by your stakeholders.

Scenario

I have attended many academic department meetings during which an administrator told a room of twenty or more faculty and staff, "Here's a new problem; how are we going to solve it?" An hour or so later, those in attendance produced ten or fifteen answers and twenty more questions about the problem.

Such an approach is counterproductive for two reasons. First, it allows everyone in the department to formulate an impression of the problem and decide on a solution based on little information. Second, trying to clarify a problem while simultaneously searching for a solution is an inefficient use of time and energy.

I. Agreeing on the Problem

Early perceptions of problems are typically broad. This is normal, as most problems go through a process of clarification. Clarifying and agreeing on the problem before trying to find a solution will help you involve the correct people in the problem-solving process and save time by focusing your efforts on the critical issues.

Depending on your departmental culture, there are three ways to approach the clarification process. The first is to have an existing departmental committee clarify the problem. It is best if the committee has oversight authority in the area where the problem has been identified, such as having the curriculum committee clarify curriculum problems.

Secondly, if the problem seems broader than a specific committee's charge, then have the departmental executive committee take up the challenge of clarifying the problem. If neither of these approaches work for your department or problem, hold a full departmental meeting to introduce the topic and ask for volunteers to form an ad hoc work group to clarify the problem. Regardless of which of these three you use, the results can be brought to a subsequent departmental meeting to fully explain the problem.

Good questions to guide clarifying process are:

- What problem are we trying to solve?

- Are we dealing with symptoms of a problem, or are we dealing with a problem that is generating the symptoms?

- How can we separate the symptoms from the problem?

- Is this a policy issue, or is this a problem with the communication of a policy?

- Is this a policy issue, or is it a problem with the application of a policy?

II. Involving the Affected People in the Solution

Once the problem is agreed upon, involve the affected people in the solution process. If the solution will affect students, involve at least one student representative in the work group, task force, or committee. Keep in mind that the student representative will not decide on what should be done, but she will provide you helpful insight.

The following chart lists groups of people who may be affected by academic decisions and suggests possible representatives to tap for service. This chart is not comprehensive, but it can guide you as you create a chart for your department. Such a chart could be included in your departmental bylaws, if appropriate for your department culture.

Affected People	Possible Representatives
Students in the program	Senior representative or club president
Faculty	Appropriate faculty committee (e.g. the executive committee)
Staff	Senior and junior staff representatives
Parents	Parent's Association chair
Staff	Chair of the leader's cabinet or advisory board

Also, I encourage you to involve departmental skeptics. When a skeptic is involved in the solution process, energy and thoughtful criticism are involved that will help everyone better understand the issues. Moreover, the skeptic will help the group submit a proposed strategy that can move forward with his/her support.

III. Agreeing to a Plan

One of the first tasks that the problem-solving work group, task force, or committee should agree to is a solution-seeking process that includes research, benchmarking, data/information collection, an analysis of results, a list of possible solutions, a way to evaluate those solutions, and a way to choose the best solution recommendation. The process affects the ultimate success of the decision, so it is essential to agree on the process, follow that process, and document the process, so that the department will have this information in the future. Starting with an agreed-upon process increases support for the final decision.

IV. Carefully Vetting the Agreed-Upon Solution

Once the group has decided on a solution and written a draft report, send the draft to as many people as appropriate and ask for feedback. Involve your departmental stakeholders in the vetting, but let another department chair, an associate dean, associate provost, or your dean (if the dean gets involved at that level) to also review the draft. These external reviews can help identify issues that were missed by your departmental group.

In terms of other reviewers, I suggest you keep your business, grants and contracts, and sponsored programs offices in mind as possible external reviewers to ensure that any proposed solutions involving these offices fit well within their policies and procedures. They may know of options and limitations the department missed.

V. Publicizing the Implementation

Implement the solution, then publicize it. Start internally and then spread outward beyond the department as appropriate. Here are some sample steps to follow:

1. Announce the solution through internal communication, like a departmental email.

2. Follow up with an email to the college leadership, alumni leaders, and/or leaders of the parents' group.

3. Follow up with appropriate communication to external stakeholders, for example through a departmental newsletter.

4. Post the solution on the appropriate web page (either password-protected or open to the public).

5. Be sure that the report and the results are archived appropriately (according to department/college practice).

Summary

Improving problem-solving processes in your department can help you avoid common issues associated with decision making in academia. The commitment to shared responsibility that lies at the heart of academic collegiality means making decisions via open and transparent processes that invite stakeholder feedback and support. The five strategies presented here can improve your departmental problem-solving processes and help garner support for the solutions.

SKILL #6: IMPROVING MEETINGS

Where Chairs Can Go Wrong

Some meetings can be a huge waste of time and effort and result in little or no collaborative gains. However, when planned and carried out properly, effective meetings can help academic administrators to better do their jobs by allowing them to work in collaboration with other members of their department--in short, meetings help us to achieve what we can't achieve on our own. However, the responsibility to ensure that meetings are effective and productive is ours and this section offers tips to ensure that meeting time is not wasted.

Common problems that chairs can face are:

- Trying to do it all alone

- Missing out on opportunities to get help

Improving the effectiveness of meetings can help chairs cope with both of these challenges by helping the chair delegate responsibilities and create an structure in which assignments can be made.

Scenario

Once a month, on a Friday afternoon at 4, a departmental chair holds a mandatory 90 minute department meeting that includes all faculty and staff. The point of the meeting is to deal with all departmental matters and concerns. The agendas for these meetings are very full, often including reports, presentations, and a dozen or more discussion items. The chair despised these meetings when he was a faculty member because they always started late, ran long, and ended with little or no progress being made toward solving departmental problems or concerns. Now, in his second year as chair, he still despises the meetings because faculty complain about the meetings, the faculty refuse to stay on topic, and he ends up doing all the work after all.

A Communication Strategies Toolbox

In order to improve the productivity of meetings, follow the acronym **TOPIC** to address five key ways to make meetings more effective:

1.   **T**ime: Start and end on time, and use meeting time wisely

2.   **O**pen: Foster a safe place for ideas and discussions

3.   **P**lan: Before, during, and after

4.   **I**ntent: Have a focus, purpose, and reason

5.   **C**ollaborate: Rather than dictate

I. Time

One reason so many people in organizations hate meetings is that they feel the meetings are a waste of time. In order to minimize this problem, start and end your meetings at the times you've indicated. End meetings early if you accomplish the agenda before the appointed end time. Since some of your committee members may have to travel from other areas of campus, be sure to factor in travel time to and from your meeting, especially if it coincides with class times. If you know that that the first morning classes on Wednesdays end at 9 a.m., you should schedule your meeting to begin at 9:05 a.m. or 9:10 a.m., in order to give faculty or students time to travel to the meeting. In general, you should attempt to schedule meetings at convenient times for the attendees.

Don't worry about canceling or rescheduling a meeting if it appears that several people can't attend, or if there is an unexpected delay in receiving materials that are important to the goals of the meeting. It's better to cancel a meeting than waste the attendees' time. Let people know as soon as possible when you need to cancel or reschedule a meeting. Give them at least twenty-four hours' notice, if possible.

Finally, manage the meeting time closely so you can accomplish the goals of the agenda within the given time period. One way to do this is to assign a certain number of minutes for each agenda item.

II. Open

Strive to make the meeting a safe place for ideas and discussions. Don't allow unnecessary criticism or negativity hamper the discussion. If someone is being overly critical or negative, try refocusing his/her attention: "We understand your criticism, Jim, and thank you for sharing. If you have something else to add, please do so. Otherwise, we need to move on," or, "I understand that you don't agree. Can you help us find a different solution?" The key to keeping the discussion open is to avoid allowing a single voice or perspective to dominate the meeting and squelch other voices and ideas.

Likewise, don't allow bullying or mobbing during the discussion. Bullying is self-explanatory; mobbing occurs when a small group of people decide their position is the only one they will allow the group to consider. As a result they don't let others state their opinions openly without a barrage of criticism. If you find yourself leading a meeting where one person is bullying others, or if a group is ganging up on an individual or another group, halt the discussion to allow the victims time to reply by saying something like, "Thank you for your comments. Let's hear from Janet and Cindy now." Your attendees will appreciate you protecting them from bullying and mobbing, and it will reinforce your commitment to an open and safe dialogue in your meetings.

In order to help some individuals be heard, you may need to ask those people specifically to state their opinions. For example, you may look around the room and say, "I haven't heard from you, Jacqueline. Is there something you would like to say?" Especially encourage the dissenters in the group to express their thoughts and concerns; I find that dissenters can be very helpful in identifying problems or "pathway potholes" that others may have overlooked.

III. Planning

It's useful to think of meetings as three stages: pre-meeting planning, the meeting, and post-meeting follow-up.

Pre-meeting planning includes all of the actions needed to provide the meeting with the best opportunity to be successful. The minimum requirement is a well-designed agenda that realistically lays out a plan for the meeting. Other effective pre-meeting resources include sending read-ahead materials to inform the attendees of important information, polls to gauge the opinions of the attendees, votes to resolve decisions, records relevant to the discussion items, and summaries of previous meetings.

During the meeting, take notes so that they can be provided those in attendance, along with a brief summary at the end of the meeting. It's also important to keep an eye on the clock and move through the agenda effectively, saving time at the end to recap, summarize, and decide on the next steps and/or assign tasks.

After the meeting, send out a summary of the discussion with appropriate reminders of what steps or tasks attendees agreed should come next.

IV. Intent

The overall intent of the meeting should be stated explicitly to the attendees. Once you have clarified the intent of the meeting, you can appropriately focus your agenda to achieve the required goals. Without clear goals, participants can become easily distracted and the meeting structure falls apart. The best way to avoid this is to understand the main intent of the meeting and design the agenda to accomplish specific goals to achieve that intent. Keep the purpose in mind and don't allow distractions from the agenda.

Of course, there are good reasons to hold general meetings; for example, it's common for departments to have an annual departmental meeting where the agenda consists of a wide range of informational items. But in these cases, the intent of the meeting is to cover informational material, not to resolve problems or work on goals. Likewise, open forums and town hall meetings may appear less structured than faculty senate meetings, but the intent of these meetings is to allow everyone the opportunity to speak their mind and ask questions.

Problems arise when a meeting that needs a focused intent is either so poorly planned or poorly managed that it becomes an unstructured gripe session, or social hour. Therefore, give the specific intent of the meeting close attention in the pre-meeting planning, and then design an agenda that will drive the meeting forward with that intent in mind.

V. Collaborate

With the exception of the general informational meetings briefly discussed above, effective meetings are not for unidirectional communication. I call unidirectional communication meetings "decree meetings" because their sole purpose seems to be issuing decrees. If the point of the meeting is to tell others what they need to do to file a leave slip, reserve the conference room on the weekend, or give them information that does not require discussion, such as the registrar's deadline for final grades, these goals can be accomplished more effectively via email. The point of having a meeting is to provide a forum for interaction and collaboration with others. If a meeting is truly effective, you will benefit from that interaction and collaboration. The collegial nature of academics requires collaboration to accomplish departmental goals, and meetings are one way to facilitate collaboration. Moreover, collaboration can build rapport with your department stakeholders.

Summary

Maybe people hate meetings because there are too many, and are often poorly planned and executed. I cannot promise that your stakeholders will enjoy your meetings, but I can ensure that your meetings will be more productive if you keep these TOPIC guidelines in mind when planning and executing them.

SKILL #7: BUILDING BUY-IN

Where Chairs Can Go Wrong

Higher education is facing tremendous pressures to innovate and economize, yet progress and change are difficult to achieve because the collegial concept of shared responsibility requires stakeholders with various interests and perspectives to come together in a shared vision to enact change. Unfortunately, busy chairs can find themselves struggling to implement change given the challenges that are endemic in higher education.

Common problems that chairs can face are:

- Underestimating challenges

- Starting with how (not why)

- Alienating people who are needed

The ability to encourage your stakeholders to buy in to change is essential to realizing effective progress in your department. Having faculty, staff, and students invested in change can lighten the chair's responsibilities and drive the change forward.

Scenario

The dean of a liberal arts college was facing decreasing enrollments as more and more students were opting for programs in Business and Engineering. She realized that one way to economize without having to cut academic programs was to target administrative costs. After much consideration, she proposed the merger of two smaller programs into one larger department, thus removing the need for two sets of program administrators.

With this in mind, she met with both program chairs and asked them to work out a merger plan with a target implementation date of the following fall semester. Unfortunately, both chairs underestimated the faculty resistance to the proposed merger and after presenting several merger proposals that their faculty rejected for various reasons, the chairs were forced to tell their dean that they had failed to achieve the support they needed for a merger plan to be successful.

A Communication Strategies Toolbox

Consider the following steps for cultivating buy-in for change in the academic unit:

1. Ask for help

2. Start with why; end with how

3. Make a plan, review, and revise

I. Ask for Help

When speaking with stakeholders about a change goal, do not downplay the complexity of the task or the difficulty of the challenge. Be honest about your perceptions of the challenge and explain the threat or opportunity that is prompting a desire for the change. If you think the change will be difficult, be honest. Talk about your perceptions and describe the concerns as you understand them. Your colleagues will appreciate knowing you understand what is involved and how hard they need to work to achieve the goal. During these discussions, invite others to express their concerns, and focus on understanding their perspective.

Once you explain your concerns and hear theirs, personalize your request for help by meeting with your stakeholders face-to-face (or at least by phone) in pairs or small groups. Do not send memos or emails soliciting help in the early stages of building stakeholder buy-in; instead use a personal approach that brings you face-to-face with your stakeholders as often as possible. If individual or small group meetings are impossible for all stakeholders, hold open forums or town hall meetings where interested stakeholders can share their thoughts and concerns. During these interactions, be open to alternatives and listen to their ideas. After you hear what they have to say, you can respond appropriately.

Moreover, identify the biggest detractors/dissenters and ask them to be engaged in the solution. A personal meeting with the most outspoken detractors will give you the opportunity to talk with them about ways they can turn their dissent into collaboration.

Once you personally communicate with everyone involved in the issue (at some level), enlist the help of your top departmental influencers to help solicit aid from your stakeholders.

By acknowledging the challenges and soliciting stakeholder help, you'll build goodwill and provide a way for everyone involved, even detractors, to play a positive role in the process.

Scenario

Three years of departmental assessment data from the basic science course sequence showed that student command of the material was positively affected by the course section (by instructor), and not by final grade in the courses. In other words, even "C" students in Dr. Goodlet's course retained more of the basic material and were, therefore, better prepared for upper level courses than "A & B" students in sections that were not taught by Dr. Goodlet. As a result, the chair formed a faculty committee to review the data and determine why Dr. Goodlet's students were better prepared. The faculty committee found that Dr. Goodlet used a standard final examination that had been developed by the discipline's national association that required the students to be able to master the important concepts that would be needed for future courses. As a result, the chair called a special meeting of the entire faculty to discuss the committee's findings and asked the faculty to decide what course of action would be best to close the gap in student success in the basic science sequence.

II. Start with Why; End with How

Linking your change goal to your unit's mission, strategic plan, and culture can help your stakeholders understand why the change is needed or desired. A key first step is to devise a precise statement of the change goal that can be easily understood and shared both internally and externally. This statement must speak to how the change goal is linked to the departmental mission or strategic plan.

Once you develop an agreed-upon statement, determine the measurable outcomes that will be used to assess progress of the goal. Determining measurable outcomes ahead of time will inform everyone of what is being measured, how it's being measured, and the goal's targets, both long term and short term. Benchmarking, or studying the progress of other departments, can help you decide what to measure and identify realistic targets. When benchmarking, it's helpful to have a list of aspirational peers to which you can compare your department's standing, progress, and proposed targets. Your university office of institutional assessment can help you understand where your department stands compared to your aspirational peers.

When everyone involved has a clear concept of the change goal as it relates to the unit's mission and they understand how to progress toward the goal and how progress will be measured, they are more likely to buy in and support the change in meaningful ways.

In the above scenario, the chair began with the why question. Why are the students in Goodlet's sections better prepared? Armed with the findings of the faculty committee, the chair asked the faculty as a whole to review and make a recommendation on how to improve student success. The ultimate decision was to use a standard final across all sections of the basic course in order to see if that move improved student success. Metrics were set using the standard assessment tools and a standard final was adopted.

III. Make a Plan, Review, and Revise

Once you establish a clear change goal, with measurable outcomes, and gain the support of many stakeholders, begin the process of developing a plan. However, do not lose sight of the fact that there are still opportunities to garner even more support as the process begins.

Evaluate your change plan and focus on the specific problems that need solving, then prioritize them and divide them up among your stakeholders. If your stakeholders see that the individual elements of the plan are less overwhelming than the overall goal, they are more likely to get on board with the process. It's understandable to see how a junior faculty member with a busy research agenda could be wary of engaging in a massive, comprehensive change plan, but she may be more comfortable with a supporting role in a single, simpler stage of the plan.

Start by identifying the easier sub goals and have your groups address these first. Success is a motivator, and once members of the department realize a few successes by achieving sub goals, they will be more motivated to take on more challenging sub goals. Be sure to set milestones within the plan, measure progress, and report on each milestone you reach. You may even be able to graphically represent the progress in an appealing way show the department progress in an ongoing visual fashion. This type of reporting can generate interest and encourage your stakeholders along the path to change.

Finally, review, revise, and revisit the plan often. Remember, tweaking the plan is acceptable. Plans are made to be reviewed and revised. Ultimately, the best plan is the one that is working.

Scenario

After careful consideration and benchmarking, the Humanities department faculty decided to implement an online tutoring program for teaching undergraduates how to avoid common plagiarism problems related to misunderstandings about the proper way to cite sources and use direct quotes. Each student received an email with a link to the program and instructions on how to complete the program. Over the course of the next two semesters, the faculty were surprised to see that academic dishonesty cases related to plagiarism did not decrease at all. The faculty could have just decided to junk the online tutorial, but instead they looked at the process and determined that email approach was not sufficient for helping the students understand the importance of the tutorials. Therefore, they revised their plan by incorporating the online tutorial into the introductory Humanities course that all majors were required to take. The result was that the students better understood the importance of the tutorial and the faculty began seeing fewer plagiarism cases.

Summary

Stakeholder buy-in equals commitment to change that will help your unit meet the growing challenges facing higher education. Change is difficult and in academia, it is nearly impossible without stakeholder buy-in. Learning to use effective communication skills to build commitment to change will increase the likelihood that your department can adapt and overcome the challenges facing higher education.

CONCLUSION

In this book, I covered seven key skills of effective communication strategies for academic administrators. Although each of these skills covered is important in itself--active listening; supportive communication; dealing with complaints; building rapport; and improving problem solving, meetings, and stakeholder buy-in-- using them together in various ways can help department heads accomplish a wide variety of goals and strategies.

If there is one key to effective communication, it is to practice these skills frequently and tailor them to your personal style and departmental culture. Your job is demanding, fast paced, and constantly evolving; using these skills until you become comfortable with them will help you deal with challenges as they occur during your day. Academic administrators frequently say that they spend their days "fighting fires," indicating that many of their daily challenges seem to pop up like a blaze, consuming all of their energy just to deal with one challenge before the next one erupts. Internalizing these effective communication skills will help you better understand and deal with problems as they arise.

Moreover, by effectively dealing with complaints and improving your ability to solve problems and build support among your departmental colleagues, you will have more time to work on the projects and initiatives that will make your department better, stronger, adaptable, and meaningfully progressive.

Ultimately, one of the most important parts of your job as an academic administrator is leadership and mentorship. Yes, the budget needs to balance, the courses must be scheduled, and there are many meetings to attend, but your success as an administrator will be determined by your ability to lead your department stakeholders effectively and mentor your colleagues, students, and staff as they grow in their roles and achieve their goals.